The Girlhood Diary of

Wanda Gág,

1908-1909:

Portrait of a Young Artist

Edited by Megan O'Hara

Content Consultant:
Gary Harm, Administrator of Wanda Gág's Estate
and Nephew of Wanda Gág

Blue Earth Books

an imprint of Capstone Press
Mankato, Minnesota

Blue Earth Books are published by Capstone Press
151 Good Counsel Drive, P.O. Box 669, Mankato, Minnesota 56002
http://www.capstone-press.com

Library of Congress Cataloging-in-Publication Data
Gág, Wanda.
    The girlhood diary of Wanda Gág, 1908-1909: portrait of a young artist / edited by Megan O'Hara.
    p. cm.—(Diaries, letters, and memoirs)
    Includes bibliographical references and index.
    ISBN 0-7368-0598-2
    1. Gág, Wanda, 1893-1946—Diaries—Juvenile literature. 2. Illustrators—United States—Diaries—
Juvenile literature. [1. Gág, Wanda, 1893-1946—Childhood and youth. 2. Illustrators. 3. Authors, American.
4. Women—Biography. 5. Diaries.] I. O'Hara, Megan. II. Title. III. Series.
NC975.5.G34 A2 2001
741.6'42'092—dc21
[B]   00-035790

Summary: The diary of Wanda Gág records her childhood experiences in school, hardships at home, and
dreams of becoming a great artist. Includes sidebars, activities, and a timeline related to this era.

Selections from Wanda Gág's diary are taken from *Growing Pains* by Wanda Gág, copyright 1940 by
Wanda Gág, renewed 1967 by Robert Janssen. Used by permission of Coward-McCann, Inc., a
division of Penguin Putnam, Inc.

Editorial Credits
Editor: Rachel Koestler
Designer: Heather Kindseth
Illustrator: Linda Clavel
Photo researchers: Heidi Schoof
    and Kimberly Danger
Artistic effects: Louise Sturm-McLaughlin

Photo Credits
Brown County Historical Society, 9 (left),
9 (middle), 12, 14, 17, 19, 20, 21, 23,
28 (bottom right); Gary Harm, 5, 6, 7, 8, 9
(right), 18 (top), 22, 24, 26, 27, 28 (bottom left),
29 (bottom); Minnesota Historical Society,
28 (top); Scott Swanson/Archive Photos, 29
(top); Gregg Andersen, 15, 18 (middle), 25

Acknowledgments
Blue Earth Books thanks Darla Gebhard from
the Brown County Historical Society for her
assistance with this book.

1 2 3 4 5 6 06 05 04 03 02 01

CONTENTS

Editor's Note

The Diaries, Letters, and Memoirs series introduces real young people from different time periods in American history. Whenever possible, the diary entries in this book appear word for word as they were written in the young person's original diary. Because the diary appears in its original form, you will notice some misspellings and mistakes in grammar. To clarify the writer's meaning, corrections or explanations within a set of brackets sometimes follow the misspellings and mistakes.

This book contains only portions of Wanda Gág's girlhood diary. Text sometimes has been removed from the individual diary entries. In these cases, you will notice three dots in a row, which are called ellipses. Ellipses show that words or sentences are missing from a text.

You can find a more complete version of Wanda's diary in the book *Growing Pains: Diaries and Drawings for the Years 1908-1917*. More information about this book is listed in the To Learn More section on page 31.

"*I was born in this country, but often feel as though I had spent my early years in Europe. My father was born in Bohemia, as were my mother's parents. My birthplace—New Ulm, Minnesota—was settled by Middle Europeans, and I grew up in an atmosphere of Old World customs and legends, of Bavarian and Bohemian folk songs, of German Märchen and Turnverein activities. I spoke no English until I went to school.*"

—*Wanda Gág, 1940*

Wanda Gág
The Girlhood Diary of a Young Artist

In 1893, Wanda Hazel Gág was born in New Ulm, Minnesota. She was the oldest of seven children. Her father had traveled to the United States from Bohemia, an area of Europe that is now the Czech Republic. Wanda's mother was born in the United States. But her mother's family also had traveled to the United States from Bohemia.

Wanda's parents were artistic. Wanda's father, Anton Gág, was a painter and photographer. Wanda's beloved "Papa" created oil paintings in his sunny attic studio. He supported the family by selling his paintings and photographs and through his decorative paintings on walls in homes and churches. Wanda's mother, Lissi Biebl, designed and sewed imaginative clothing and costumes for the children. As Anton's photo assistant, she also became a gifted photographer. Lissi brought artistic touches to everyday life by crafting lacy valentines and shaping extra bread dough into tiny books. The children split the bread books open and spread them with butter.

Wanda's parents encouraged their children to be creative. They stopped their work to pay special attention to the children's drawings or to answer their questions. Wanda and her siblings began to draw as soon as they could hold a pencil.

The Gág children posed in this 1904 picuture. From left to right in the back row stand Stella, Dehli, and Wanda. Howard, Asta, and Thusnelda (Tussy) sit in the front row. The baby, Flavia, is not pictured.

Wanda's life changed forever when she was 15 years old. Anton became sick with tuberculosis. Wanda stayed home from school to help with household chores and the children so her mother could care for him. On his deathbed, Anton took hold of Wanda's hand and uttered, "What Papa couldn't do, Wanda will have to finish." These words inspired Wanda to develop her artistic talents. On May 22, 1908, Anton died. Wanda's mother was left to support the children. The youngest was just 1 year old.

Lissi became sick shortly after Anton's death and was confined to her bed much of the time. Although only a teenager, Wanda did much of the cooking, cleaning, and caring for her young siblings. People in her small town told her to forget about education and art and concentrate on finding a job to support the family.

Wanda's mother and father were married in 1892.

Wanda insisted on pursuing her goals. "I have a right to go on drawing. I will not be a clerk. And we are all going through high school," she said. Despite Wanda's heavy household responsibilities, she found time to create portraits, sketches, poems, and stories. She submitted her work to the "Journal Junior." This section of a Minneapolis newspaper was devoted to the artworks and writings of young people.

Wanda discovered an old ledger of her father's accounts. She decided to keep track of expenses and earnings for her artworks, just as Anton had done. Soon her thoughts, hopes, and dreams found their way into these notebooks. Wanda's writings provide a glimpse into the mind and heart of an artistic girl and her determination to follow her dream.

The Diary of Wanda Gág

Monday, Oct. 12, 1908—

I sent one of my pictures to the Journal Junior, "Toddie's Hanged Our Dollies," and forgot to put my address on it so I sent another envelope with my address on it. The same day I sent a story, "Lou's Soap Bubble Party," and a picture to illustrate it, to McCall's. Some time ago I sent these three articles to the Youth's Companion–

        Story—Golden Brooch
        Picture—Great Grandmother's Chest
        Poem—   "   "   "

I wonder how the whole thing will turn out.

A few days ago Margaret Kelly told me that Martha Schmid didn't believe I drew free hand. She thinks I trace. Trace indeed! When I don't even care much for copying.

Tuesday, Oct. 13—

Some time ago I got a check for $1.00 prize from the Woman's Home Companion for a drawing. It had 14 children on it. I got the dollar at the Citizen's Bank.

I'm thru reading "Kristy's Rainy Day Party" and quite done with the Orange Fairy Book.

It is a beautiful day.

I do hope May Harris Anson [editor of the Journal Junior] will not throw

Wanda drew many self-portraits to practice her skills. While attending St. Paul School of Art, she often hung a coat over her window after curfew and sketched her reflection by candlelight into the early morning hours.

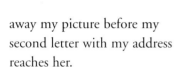

"A WINDY DAY"

away my picture before my
second letter with my address
reaches her.

The baby can say Deya for Stella, Dudi
for Tussy, Adda for Asta, Deyi for Dehli
and all kinds of other words that she learns
every day.

The same day I was at the bank I got
our Fair money for this and last year,
$3.25 in all.

1907	Wanda Drawing—1st	$.50
	Dehli and Asta drawing—1st	$.50
	Tussy pillow slip—2nd	$.25
1908	Wanda drawing—1st	$.50
	Dehli " —1st	$.50
	Wanda " —3rd	$.25
	Stella Splasher—2nd	$.25
	Tussy centerpiece—1st	$.50

*Wanda drew placecards and
postcards to sell. She also
drew sketches of her siblings
and illustrations to submit
to magazines and
fair contests.*

My money from the Fair and the one dollar from the Women's Home
Companion will go for shoes, I think.

School is going out now. We'll have pot pie for dinner.

Draw a Profile Face

The Gág children learned to draw at a young age. They often drew people they knew. You can use some basic guidelines to draw a face, and then add your own details. Change the eyes, hair, and other features to look like someone you know. If people will not sit and pose for you, use a photograph to closely observe their features.

What You Need

one large piece of paper, either plain or with a graph pattern on it
one #2 lead pencil or #3 lead pencil
an eraser

What You Do

1. Draw a shape like an egg with the narrow end pointed downward at an angle.
2. Draw faint, horizontal lines through the shape to mark the position of the eye, nose, ear, and mouth. Make two horizontal lines almost halfway down the face to mark the place for the eye and ear. Below these lines, draw another horizontal line to mark the nose. Near the bottom of the shape, draw a line to mark the spot for the mouth.
3. Draw in the eye, nose, ear, and mouth shapes as shown.
4. Smooth the angles to look like facial curves.
5. Erase the horizontal construction lines.
6. Fill in the features with some simple shading lines. Near the inside corner of the eye, lightly shade the side of the nose. Shade the center of the eye. Shade a half circle below the mouth to suggest the chin. Draw some curved marks and lines for the hair and eyebrows.

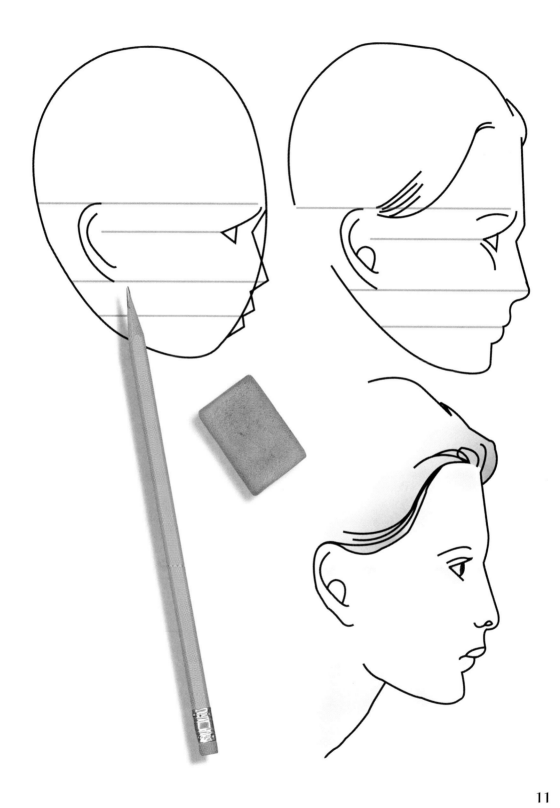

Thursday, Oct. 15. A splendid day.—

I finished the story yesterday and started another one.

Mama lay down this afternoon, and is still in bed . . .

I made supper tonight. We had fried potatoes, left over cabbage, and a little bit of veal-stew. We took mama's supper up on the waiter [tray]. The baby slept twice. I ironed a little today.

Saturday, Oct. 17. A dreary day.—

Made another picture, "When sister makes the candy."

Yesterday grandma sent up two chickens, some cabbage, carrots and three cheese-cakes.

Stella made up a poem about a leaf last night, and Thursday night I wrote 2 poems, "The Snowstorm" and "A Mother Goose Party." Here is "The Snowstorm."

I.   I go to bed with my candle-light.
Outside the world is solemn and white,
And quietly, softly, hushed and slow,
Come the pretty, white little flakes of snow.
    And leaving the world so calm and so white,
    I creep to bed in the peaceful night.

2.   In the morning when I get up, Oh ho!
The world is full of the drifting snow!
The little red house way down by the hills,
Is drifted with snow to its window sills.
    I meet the world in the early morn,
    In a jolly, frollicky wild snowstorm!

. . . I was at Ione Dekker's and got the Oct. Woman's Home Companion. Am writing the story of a Hallowe'en party to send them. Asta wrote a story too. It's just too funny! The baby is still up. She isn't sleepy yet. We have to laugh so much at her. She can say book, Aggaga for Egg-O-See and wawa for water. She can chew gum nicely.

They say the biggest mill in Minneapolis is burning. They also say that the woods in Michigan are burning.

I sketched the baby tonight after school, and just a little while before I sketched Asta 4 times and Dehli 3 times. I sketched them in a dark room. They wore a night gown and held a candle. I want one for "The Snowstorm." 2 of them are in India Ink. The others are in pencil. I wish I had a decent pencil . . .

Today was "leaf-searching" day. I got the *most* leaves and the prettiest ones, too; plum leaves, apple tree leaves, raspberry bush leaves, rose bush leaves, maple leaves and any number of other kinds. I have two shoe boxes full and a capful, and one of the buggy pockets is full too. Aunt Magdalene was here . . . Had sago pudding tonight. Good night.

Oct. 23. Rain, Rain, Rain.—

Fern Fischer and Judy Dekker were over here last night. I made Judy a paper doll and Fern a picture. Washed and dried the breakfast dishes today and washed the dinner dishes. Today is ironing day and ironing night too it seems.

I made the first illustration to "The Snowstorm" tonight, that is, put in the shadings, etc. Wish I had somebody to tell me what they think about it. Somebody that knows about art. Stella is too young to criticise. No mail for me. It's perfectly discouraging. Wish I could draw like Mary True Ayer.

One of baby Flavia's first words was Egg-O-See. This 1908 postcard shows an advertisement for Egg-O-See, a popular breakfast cereal in the early 1900s.

"Dere aint go'ner be no leavins"

Oct. 26, Monday. Rain, Rain, Rain.—

Rain since Friday *more* or *less*. Saturday we worked most of the time. Not much time for reading, drawing or anything like that. Yesterday I was over at Dekker's in the evening with Stella. Wore the white and pink lawn dress. We had apple dumplings for our Sunday dinner, and sour fish for supper tonight. We bought him of Mr. Schmid for 15 cents. For dinner we had beef steak fried in the furnace. Copied pretty many [of my] stories and poems the day before yesterday, and Sunday I started to copy a fairy story [of my own]. No drawing worth mentioning.

Mama was up at Helk's today. I cleaned up part of the children's side of the attic today. They've mussed it all up. I gave Tussy a bundle of cloth to sew with today.

Wanda took care of her younger siblings. She is shown here at age 10 holding Howard.

Nov. 2. A fine, warm, sunny day.—

My hopes are shattered some. Got a letter from the Youth's Companion with my stuff in it . . .

Fern Fischer was here yesterday and she said that somebody told her I don't do anything but read and draw. I guess so! I wonder if washing dishes, sweeping about 6 times a day, picking up things the baby and Howard throw around are reading.

And I've never heard of taking care of babies, combing little sisters, cleaning bed rooms & attics as being classed as drawing!

I wonder what else people will say about me.

Yesterday night I drew and inked 12 postals [postcards] and today I colored them. They are all for Thanksgiving & I think I'll ask Eggen's Drug Store if they don't want to buy any of me . . .

Making Spaetzle

Spaetzle is a German dish that Wanda's family sometimes prepared. These small dumplings usually are served with sauerkraut or seasoned beef.

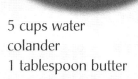

What You Need

2 eggs
medium bowl
fork
wooden spoon
liquid measuring
  cup
½ cup water
measuring
  spoons

¼ teaspoon
  baking powder
½ teaspoon salt
dry-ingredient
  measuring cups
1½ cups flour
large saucepan
  with lid

5 cups water
colander
1 tablespoon butter

What You Do

1. In medium bowl, beat two eggs with a fork.
2. Stir ½ cup water, ¼ teaspoon baking powder, ½ teaspoon salt, and 1½ cups flour into beaten eggs. Mix well.
4. Bring 5 cups of water to a boil in saucepan.
5. One teaspoon at a time, drop pieces of flour mixture into boiling water.
6. Cover and simmer 15 minutes. Do not lift cover while cooking.
7. Drain water from spaetzles using colander.
8. Return spaetzles to saucepan.
9. On low heat, melt 1 tablespoon butter in spaetzles.

Makes about 8 servings

Nov. 11, Wed. A cold, bright day.—

Miss Meadows [a high school teacher] asked me whether I was going somewhere to study art later, and I told her I'd like to go to high school first. "All right, come in January," she said. But I don't know whether I can. To be sure I'd like to but—. Ione Dekker said that I should take 4 half subjects & so get 2 credits.

I've got Tussy's Christmas presents done—two of them—bookmarks.

I and Stella and Asta were out at Aunt Klaus's. We got a lot of pretty milkweeds & rose berries & autumn leaves, besides some apples which Aunt Klaus gave us along. We had a splendid time.

I drew a heading in india ink for Aunt Janet's Pages [a children's section of the *Woman's Home Companion* magazine] but I don't know whether I'll send it—the stamps are giving out, that's why. My india ink is quite gone too. I don't see how I'm to get some when it's gone.

I phoned to Eggen's Drug Store several days ago and asked what they intended to do about the postals and they said they'd keep them. He said they'd sold quite a number already.

November 12. A cold day. It's snowing.—

Mama didn't feel well so I made supper. We didn't have much to make anyway, just bacon and potatoes to fry. Made a Fireplace Picture last night. I'd like to send it to the Journal Junior, but the stamps—.

Nov. 13. A cold snowy day. Friday.—

Great good luck! I found an old book with 5 stamps—2 cent stamps—in it! I'm so glad. Now I'm going to send the Heading for Aunt Janet's Pages, and one or two pictures to the Journal Junior . . .

Nov. 15, Sunday—

Good luck!!!!!!!!

I just got the Journal Junior from Fern, and my picture, "Toddie's Hanged Our Dollies," is in it! I suppose the dollar prize will come pretty soon. Oh I'm so glad. That makes another dollar for mama. I promised to draw Miss Brown a picture and she promised to give me a 2 cent stamp to send the Heading for Aunt Janet's Pages away. I'm glad. Asta's drawing a picture tonight. The baby can hug, kiss, show us where her heart is, and show us her tongue.

A New Ulm resident bought this postcard, which Wanda drew in 1908.

Nov. 18—

A beautiful day but oh! so twisted! Mama bought wood today—$8½ a cord. I wasn't good today, I read too much and didn't work enough. But really I wish I hadn't been so bad.

Stella, Tussy & Asta are over by Fischer's this evening, and I and mama cried.

Nov. 27—

I have been down at grandma's. We came home yesterday in time for the Thanksgiving dinner. We had pumpkin pie, potatoes, goose & apples. Oh I was homesick the last day I was at grandma's . . .

I went down to Eggen's to get some paints. I got *Devoe* with 2 yellow, 1 blue, 1 red, & also 5 Calendars at 1 cent a piece. I sell postals to Eggen's, 6 for 25 cents & they sell them for 5 cents straight thru. That makes $.75 credit for our school books, the cost of all was $1.13 I believe. I'll have that paid off pretty soon.

Aunt Magdalene was here. She brought me a blue velvet hat and promised me a black and white checked jumper. I'm so glad! . . .

December 7, Monday. A cold but bright day.—

December 4th was Dehli's birthday. She didn't get anything from us because we didn't have enough time & money to give her anything. Perhaps Asta and Tussy made her some pictures or cards tho.

Oh but I worked this afternoon. I was pegging away at copying a story with the *most horrid* pen. It scratched just like everything. It made me so cross and it was almost a thousand words long, too. I had the baby upstairs with me, too, while I was writing it. She kept climbing on my chair and begging for candy. Finally I had it done, it was the story about the "Punken Hunt" with two boys in it called Fletcher and Buster.

I sent it to the J.J. [Journal Junior]. I wanted to illustrate it at first—because several years ago I sent one too, illustrated & the Editor said I should send another one illustrated on unruled paper (I had my picture on ruled ink paper) but I've never tried it since then—but I didn't have enough time so I sent it off without . . .

December 23, Wednesday—

Oh goody! goody! goody! We've gotten so many Xmas presents. Monday they started in coming . . . On Monday, too, we got some apples but we haven't the least idea where they came from. The next day we got more apples, almost a bushel, from the Turn-verein and a great big box of underwear from Mrs. Graf. I had sent a present to her too. Today we got 100 lbs. [45 kilograms] of flour from the Ladies' Turner Society. Yesterday I was downtown with Aunt Mary and she bought just piles of things for us. The others didn't see them tho, yet . . .

Today we washed dishes and cleaned up a little and off I started for Mrs. Harrington's. Mrs. Joliffe was there when I came . . . I had noticed several pretty oil paintings in the room and was quite sure that papa had made them. Mr. Harrington told me that papa had made them, and the decorations of the room too. He said he was sorry that papa was not living. He said it was so hard to get anyone to do the decorating. Of course I had to cry. I tried to keep the tears from coming but I couldn't. I sat as if in a dream. I don't know, I felt so funny, but I found Mr. Harrington leading me into the dining room with his arm around me. I managed to stop crying just enough that I could see straight but it took pretty long for the tears to clear away . . .

Grandma Folks

Wanda and her siblings often visited their grandmother's farm. They referred to their relatives at the farm as Grandma Folks. The farm was an hour's walk along the railroad tracks, past the bustle of Goosetown. This neighborhood of New Ulm lay along the Minnesota River. Noisy gaggles of geese gave the neighborhood its nickname. Many residents kept geese to use their down feathers in making quilts and pillows.

The Grandma Folks included Grandma Biebl, Aunt Mary, Uncle Frank, Uncle Josie, and Aunt Magadalene (Lena), all of whom lived on the family farm. Aunt Mary and Aunt Lena told stories, sang songs, and played imaginative games with the children. Their aunts also taught them how to sew and cook. Uncle Frank was a craftsman who made his own tools for repairing musical instruments and furniture. Uncle Josie created drawings and watercolors, built birdhouses and furniture from willow stems, and made toys for the children. The children's favorite toy was the carousel Uncle Josie made, complete with horses, a music box, seats, and a crank to make it turn.

Grandma Biebl's house

19

Wanda and her sisters stood in their backyard in front of the garden house in 1903.

December 31. A Happy New Year!—
This is Sylvester Eve, and we children have been dripping candle.

We got coal today and the whole house is black. In the cellar the whole table and floor are as black as ink.

I brought papa's oil painting of roses up to Hershl's for the Turnverein [Turner Society]. It is a New Year's present. We had oysters, crackers, coffee, apple cake, and cinnamon cake for supper as a special New Year's treat. I don't know whether we'll stay up until midnight.

February ? Friday [1909]—
This is just an awful snowstorm, but beautiful! Why the world is a regular fairy land! Our garden house looks as clean and dainty as any fairy castle, I think, for the whole floor is covered with snow. The evergreens in Logan's garden are just laden down with thick ridges of pearly snow, and big white mountains can be seen almost everywhere. I & Tussy went to get the milk. We were dressed quite warm, with shawls over our faces, but still the wind took our breath away. I rather enjoyed it though, for some reason, I don't know why. I think it is because the landscape is so beautiful.

. . . Today is the basket ball game I guess, the high school against some other team. They're going to write the high school yells on the board today. By the way, have I said already that I'm going to high school? I am, and what's more, I'm going in the forenoon and the afternoon! Last year I went only in the afternoon. I have Miss Meadows for Rhetoric, Miss Dillon for Ancient History & English Composition, and Mr. Jellick for physical Geography.

German and Bohemian Traditions

Many residents in New Ulm had strong German and Bohemian roots. Community members preserved their culture through festivals and theater productions. Wanda and her family followed many traditions from their heritage. They cooked German and Bohemian foods, told folk tales, and celebrated holidays with fun activities.

Wanda and her sisters celebrated the Feast of St. Barbara on December 4th. Young girls hurried into the garden and broke a small branch off a fruit tree early in the morning of St. Barbara's Eve. As they broke the branch, they made a silent wish. They then placed the branch in a vase of water. If the branch bloomed by Christmas, the wish was believed to come true.

Another Bohemian tradition was lace making. This Bohemian woman is using bobbins to weave lace.

Oct. 24. A bright sunny day, cold nevertheless.—

My hands are full of blisters & sores from chopping wood. I'm always trying to make firewood but I'm afraid I'm making only chips. Then Stella broke the ax. That was the culminating point. Just about all I could chop with the hatchet was splinters.

I have made almost 5 dozen Hallowe'en cards for Miss Gerber. I only, only hope that I may go to "Beverly of Graustark" when that comes. I'll bet I'd just about jump out of my slippers for joy if I could. They're so loose anyway, it wouldn't be impossible. I feel rather glum. Trouble before, and trouble beyond, and fun at the sides only. Dreamt about school last night. I could almost cry myself sick sometimes to think that so many girls who have the opportunity of going thru High School just hate school and look upon it as hard work; while I have to be afraid any time that I may have to stop school before I know it.

Nov. 26, Friday—

The orchestra played and the Glee Club sang at the program. I read my story and got the point. Some of those Freshmen have more nerve than they ought to have. During the program one of the Freshman boys sat in my seat and when I went back to my seat he said, "That's a fine diary." I said, "Diary?" and then I caught on; they had been reading *you*, Diary! Wish you could speak so I'd know what parts they read. There is one advantage— I guess a person who isn't used to my writing can't read half of this stuff . . .

Dec. 16—

I did feel better to-day, and perhaps our little money will reach to some extent. We didn't have much of an Ancient Lesson to-day. Miss Dillon lectured. She said exactly the same thing which I've been thinking of ever & ever so often: That some children don't realize what an advantage it is to go to school. I'll confess I dream away some of the time sometimes, but then I'm generally dreaming useful things . . .

Ladies' Turner Society

In the 1800s and 1900s, women often organized into small groups, or societies, to do charitable work for their communities. These groups focused their efforts on helping widows, orphans, the sick, or the elderly.

The Ladies' Turner Society in New Ulm supported the Turnverein, or Turner Society. Turner Society members, or Turners, believed in developing strong minds through a good education and strong bodies through vigorous physical exercise. Turner societies offered gymnastic courses for men, women, and children. The Turner Society in New Ulm preserved the residents' German language and traditions by staging theater productions.

Turner Ladies exercising in 1908

"Under the mistletoe."
By WANDA HAZEL GAY.

Dec. 24, Friday—

. . . This morning I did housework, and then went to see if I had any mail. Did I? Here:—A postal from Daisy, a dollar from Prenzel's, and a check from the J.J. for 2 accepted articles. Talk of being tickled! Went down town and got mama a Christmas present (from my own money) cloth for a waist. To-night! Oh ho! Behold Santa in a blue skirt all out of press and a nonentical [not enticing] waist, stout shoes and an "ear to ear" grin. You will recognize me readily, I am sure, especially if I would have mentioned a silly nose . . .

Dec. 31, Friday—

The last day of 1909! A year, and what did it do? All kinds of things, pleasant and—some not so very pleasant. I went to school, and I am—oh so glad! I only, only hope that I may go thru High School, and I hope our good teachers will stay longer.

Uncle Frank is playing on the guitar, such sweet, clear, free music. I love to read or draw or write while I'm listening to music, so I take advantage of it now—and—write.

It is after eleven now, going pretty near to next year. School won't start until next year, which would be a deplorable fact if next year wouldn't be so very near! I shall try to make the next year a brighter one, a more interesting one, and one— that is, if it's possible—in which I have done something worthy of myself.

Oh dear, what have I done? Next to nothing. Compare my drawings to those of Jessie W. Smith, J. M. Flagg, H. C. Christy and all the rest. What are they? Why, they're noughts, zeros, nothing, against them. I've often thought of this but never wrote it down. I wonder whether I'm making any progress at all, and whether I'll be clever enough to earn much money, at least enough to make us all comfortable. I wish I could see and talk with such artists as Jessie Wilcox Smith, and Mr. Fisher, and Mr. Flagg and the rest of my favorite artists.

About 10 minutes to next year.

Starting Your Own Diary

Wanda wrote about her daily chores, education, and artwork. She shared her thoughts and feelings about her success as an artist and the financial hardship her family suffered. In her dairy, Wanda wrote about her family, friends, teachers, and local events. All of these subjects are great topics for a journal. You can keep a journal to record your life and what happens in the world each day.

What You Need

Paper: Use a blank book, a diary with a lock, or a notebook. Choose your favorite.

Pen: Choose a special pen or use different pens. You might want to use different colors to match your different moods.

Private time: Some people write before they fall asleep. Others write when they wake up. Be sure you have time to put down your thoughts without interruptions.

What You Do

1. Begin each entry in your diary with the day and date. This step helps you remember when things happened. You can go back and read about what you did a week ago, a month ago, or a year ago.
2. Write about anything that interests you. Write about what you did today. Describe whom you saw, what you studied, and songs you heard.
3. Write about your feelings. Describe what makes you happy or sad. Give your opinions about things you see, hear, or read.
4. Write in your diary regularly.

Afterword

Wanda finished high school in 1912 and later studied at the St. Paul School of Art and the Minneapolis Art School. During the years of her schooling, Wanda returned to New Ulm each summer to help her family.

In 1917, Lissi died, and Wanda and her sisters took on financial responsibility for the family. Wanda received a scholarship to attend the New York Art Students League. She earned extra income by selling her artwork to magazines. She sent money to her sisters and brother in New Ulm as often as she could. Wanda continued to help support them until they could support themselves.

The Weyhe Gallery in New York City held Wanda's first major art show in 1926. The show was a great success. With the money she earned from the show, Wanda bought a farm in New Jersey that she named "All Creation."

An editor from Coward McCann, a leading book publisher, noticed Wanda's work. The editor asked Wanda to write and illustrate a children's book. In 1928, Wanda published the children's classic, *Millions of Cats*.

Wanda posed for her high school graduation picture in 1912.

Wanda's cat, Snoopy, served as a model for many of her illustrations.

During the next 18 years, Wanda produced many artworks and children's books. Her books included *The Funny Thing* (1929), *Snippy and Snappy* (1931), and *The ABC Bunny* (1933). In 1940, Wanda published her early diaries under the title *Growing Pains*. The Weyhe Gallery held a show in honor of Wanda's achievements the same year, titled "Wanda Gág: 35 years of Picture Making."

In 1943, Wanda married Earle Humphreys. Two years later, doctors diagnosed Wanda with advanced lung cancer. She continued to write and draw during the following months when her health permitted. Wanda Gág died in June of 1946 at the age of 53. Today, Wanda is remembered as an artist, author, and illustrator. Her artwork hangs in museums all around the world.

Timeline

Henry Ford introduces the first Model I.

The United States enters World War I.

1893	1908	1912	1917

Wanda Hazel Gág is born on March 11 in New Ulm, Minnesota.

Anton Gág dies on May 22. Wanda begins her diary at age 15.

Wanda graduates from New Ulm High School.

Lissi Gág dies on January 31. Wanda begins art studies in New York after receiving a scholarship.

The 19th Amendment to the constitution gives women the right to vote.

On October 29th, Black Tuesday, the stock market crashes. The Great Depression begins.

Japanese forces bomb Pearl Harbor. The U.S. enters World War II (1939–1945).

| 1919 | 1928 | 1929 | 1940 | 1941 | 1946 |

Wanda's art is shown at Weyhe Gallery in New York. *Millions of Cats* is published.

Wanda publishes her diaries under the title *Growing Pains*.

Wanda dies on June 27.

Words to Know

cord (KORD)—a stack of wood that measured 4 feet long by 4 feet wide by 8 feet tall (1.2 meters long by 1.2 meters wide by 2.4 meters high)

deplorable (di-PLOR-uh-buhl)—horrible or terrible

determination (di-tur-min-AY-shuhn)—making a decision to accomplish something and not changing your mind

enticing (en-TYS-ing)—appealing

glee club (GLEE KLUHB)—a choir that sings short pieces

illustrate (IL-uh-strate)—to draw pictures for a book, story, or magazine

orchestra (OR-kuh-struh)—a large group of musicians who play different instruments and perform in concerts

siblings (SIB-lings)—brothers and sisters

tuberculosis (tu-bur-kyuh-LOH-siss)—a bacterial disease of the lungs

Internet Sites

Brown County Historical Society
http://www.newulmweb.com/citylights/
museum/museum.htm

Minnesota Historical Society
http://www.mnhs.org

**Language of the Land Project: A
Children's Classic: Millions of Cats**
http://www.mnbooks.org/lol/
au2-knh.htm

**Travels through Germany: German
Traditions**
http://www.travelsthroughgermany.com/
website2/traditions.htm

To Learn More

Gág, Wanda. *Growing Pains*. St. Paul: Minnesota Historical Society Press, 1984.

Gág, Wanda. *Millions of Cats*. New York: Penguin Putnam Books, 1996.

Hoyle, Karen Nelson. *Wanda Gág*. New York: Twayne Publishers, 1994.

Scott, Alma. *Wanda Gág: The Story of an Artist*. Minneapolis: University of Minnesota
Press, 1949.

Winnan, Audur H. *Wanda Gág: A Catalogue Raisonné of the Prints*. Minneapolis:
University of Minnesota Press, 1999.

Places to Write and Visit

Brown County Historical Museum
2 North Broadway
New Ulm, MN 56073

The Weyhe Gallery
101 West 57th Street
New York, NY 10019

Children's Literature Research Collections
Kerlan Collection
University of Minnesota
Minneapolis, MN 55455

Wanda Gág House
226 North Washington Street
New Ulm, MN 56073

INDEX